Ripley's Believe It or Not!®

Developed and produced by Ripley Publishing Ltd

This edition published and distributed by:
Mason Crest Publishers Inc.
370 Reed Road, Broomall, Pennsylvania 19008
(866) MCP-BOOK (toll free)
www.masoncrest.com

Ripley's Believe it or Not!
Weird and Wonderful
ISBN 978-1-4222-2029-0 (hardcover)
ISBN 978-1-4222-2063-4 (paperback)

Library of Congress Cataloging-in-Publication data is available

Ripley's Believe it or Not!—Complete 16 Title Series
ISBN 978-1-4222-2014-6

1st printing
10 9 8 7 6 5 4 3 2 1

Library of Congress Cataloging-in-Publication Data is available.
Printed in USA

PUBLISHER'S NOTE
While every effort has been made to verify the accuracy of the entries in this book, the
Publisher's cannot be held responsible for any errors contained in the work. They would
be glad to receive any information from readers.

WARNING
Some of the stunts and activities in this book are undertaken by experts and should not
be attempted by anyone without adequate training and supervision.

Ripley's Believe It or Not!

Expect... The Unexpected

WEIRD & WONDERFUL

Mason Crest Publishers

WEIRD & WONDERFUL

Oh, the oddities. The most amazing art,

outrageous festivals, and bizarre bodies are

packed into this extraordinary book. Meet the

father and son with 12 digits on each hand,

the artist who paints using his own beard, and

the men and women who participate in the

Bug Eating Championships.

*Tyler Fyre is tied in a straitjacket and hung upside
down by his ankles 6 ft (2 m) above the stage...*

BrEaD HeaD

KITTIWAT UNARROM makes edible human heads and torsos out of dough! His workplace looks like a mortuary or a serial killer's dungeon, but it is in fact a bakery.

Visitors to Unarrom's workshop near Bangkok are alarmed to see the heads and torsos lined up on shelves, and rows of arms and hands hanging from meat hooks. The Thai art student, whose family runs a bakery, uses anatomy books and his memories of visiting a forensics museum to create the human body parts. In addition to heads crafted from bread, chocolate, raisins, and cashews, he makes human arms and feet, and chicken and pig parts, incorporating red food coloring for extra bloody effect. "When people see the bread, they don't want to eat it," he says. "But when they taste it, it's just normal bread. The lesson is, don't judge by appearances."

His macabre project started out as the centerpiece of his final dissertation for his Master of Arts degree, but as word spread about his novelty-shaped bread, regular orders began coming in from the curious or from pranksters who want to surprise their friends.

Basing the models on pictures from anatomy books, Thai art student Kittiwat Unarrom lovingly creates lifelike human heads from bread. Not surprisingly, most people think twice before eating the heads.

Some of Kittiwat's creations are really gruesome and would not look out of place in a chamber of horrors. And if they're not bloody enough, he adds red food coloring to increase the effect.

When customers first saw Kittiwat's room of realistic-looking human body parts, they were shocked and thought he was crazy.

Let it Be

This toilet paper, auctioned at a starting price of £40,000, was removed from the toilets in the EMI studios at Abbey Road, London, England, when the Beatles refused to use it, objecting to its hardness and shininess. They were also said to have disliked the fact that EMI was stamped on every sheet.

The toilet paper, still on its original 1960s roll, was framed in a glass box.

Self-liposuction

Believe it or not, Yugoslav-born plastic surgeon Dimitrije Panfilov performed liposuction on himself to remove a double chin!

Tiny Letters

In 2004, physicists at Boston College, Massachussetts, managed to carve miniscule letters into a single strand of human hair. Using a laser, they created letters that were 15 micrometers tall. The technique can form items a thousand times smaller than the diameter of a human hair.

Miracle Birth

Nhlahla Cwayita was born healthy at Cape Town, South Africa, in 2003, despite developing in her mother's liver. She was only the fourth baby in the world to survive such a pregnancy.

▶ On a Shoestring

Big Bear City, California, is home to The Shoe Tree—no one quite knows how it started, but the tree continues to accumulate shoe upon shoe. Local police tried to prevent the tree being used in this way by removing all the shoes and fencing off the area, but by the next morning it was covered once again.

Circus Club

At one of the world's strangest nightclubs, the California Institute of Abnormalarts, you can dance the night away in the company of the remains of a dead clown, the stuffed carcass of a piglet-Chihuahua hybrid, a mummified arm, and such weird exhibits as Octopus Girl! The museum and nightclub is run by Carl Crew and Robert Ferguson, who collect circus memorabilia.

Bearded Lady

Vivian Wheeler has a weird claim to fame—she is the woman with the world's longest beard. Wheeler, who comes from Wood River, Illinois, was born with facial hair, having inherited a genetic hormonal disorder from her mother. Her father refused to accept her beard and forced her to shave it off from the age of seven, but she later traveled with sideshow acts under the stage name of Melinda Maxie, dying her natural red hair black for greater impact. Her full beard has now reached a length of 11 in (28 cm), although she usually wears it tied up.

Bead Art

Liza Lou of Topanga, California, used 40 million glass beads to create a kitchen and garden that was first displayed at the Kemper Museum of Contemporary Art in Kansas City in 1998. If the beads had been strung together, they would have stretched about 380 mi (610 km), the same distance as that between Los Angeles and San Francisco.

Two-faced Kitten

A kitten was born in Glide, Oregon, in June 2005, with two faces! Gemini astounded vets and owner Lee Bluetear with her two mouths, two tongues, two noses, and four eyes. Sadly, she died within a week.

Sentimental Value

Ezekiel Rubottom decided to keep his left foot after it was amputated in 2005! He stored it in the front porch of his Kansas home. After neigbors complained, he said "I'm not sick, I just wanted my foot."

Mark Hostetler, an ecologist at the UNIVERSITY OF FLORIDA, has written a book on how to identify **insect splats** left on your car. The book is titled *That Gunk On Your Car.*

⛰ Burning Passion

To demonstrate his love for his girlfriend, Todd Grannis set himself on fire before going down on one knee and asking her to marry him! Wearing a cape soaked in gasoline, Grannis, 38, climbed a 10-ft (3-m) scaffold at Grants Pass, Oregon, in July 2005. After being set on fire, he plunged into a swimming pool and told stunned sweetheart Malissa Kusiek: "Honey, you make me hot ... I'm on fire for you." After such a stunt, she had to say yes!

Bird Poop

Believe it or not, an American firm offers individually crafted models of birds made from genuine Californian horse dung!

Faking for Fun

Chaucey Shea of St. Catherine's, Ontario, has a potentially illegal hobby. He has mastered more than 2,000 forgeries of famous signatures, including English playwright William Shakespeare, and several presidents of the United States.

Seat of Learning

Bill Jarrett, a retired artist from Grand Rapids, Michigan, has been studying toilet paper for the past 30 years and now boasts a vast collection of tissue-related memorabilia.

Wacky Wedding

At a wedding in Calgary, Alberta, Canada, in 1998, the bride was a sword swallower, the groom tamed bees, and the maid of honor made a living eating live bugs and worms! Megan Evans married Jim Rogers (Calgary's "Bee Man") in front of 200 musicians and freak-show performers, including worm-loving bridesmaid Brenda Fox.

◀ Half-size Jeanie

Born without any legs, Jeanie Tomaini achieved fame in U.S. sideshows as "The Half Girl." While on tour, Jeanie, who is 2 ft 6 in (0.76 m), married Al, who stood 8 ft 4 in (2.54 m) tall and wore size 22 shoes. They went on to form a successful act as "The World's Strangest Couple."

All Fingers and Thumbs
Filipinos Albert M. Perculeza and his son Karl Cedric each have 12 digits on their hands and 12 digits on their feet (see below). All 48 digits are fully functional.

Ash Art
Bettye Jane Brokl incorporates the ashes of dead people into abstract paintings. The Biloxi, Mississippi, artist sprinkles the cremation ashes on the artwork to create a pictorial memorial for a loved one.

There's no *fast food* at **June**, a new restaurant in LAKEWOOD RANCH, FLORIDA. The **nine-course** meals take four hours to eat.

Gerbil Installation
An artist from Newcastle, England, made her pet gerbil the star of a 2005 exhibition. "The Gerbil's Guide to the Galaxy" showed Sally Madge's rodent chewing its way through a 1933 edition of the *New Illustrated Universal Reference Book*, "choosing" certain words to eat.

Fiberglass Shell
A mud turtle that had its shell broken into eight pieces by cars in Lutz, Florida, was given a new fiberglass one in 1982.

Junk Exhibition
In 2005, an exhibition in London, England, by Japanese artist Tomoko Takahashi featured 7,600 pieces of junk. The exhibits included old washing machines, broken toys, a rusty muck-spreader, and three stuffed blackbirds.

Love Shack
In April 2005, a building was covered in 6,000 love letters, some penned by international celebrities, as part of the annual Auckland Festival in New Zealand.

Mind Reader
Matthew Nagle, of Weymouth, Massachusetts, has a brain chip that reads his mind. Severely paralyzed after being stabbed in the neck in 2001, he has a revolutionary implant that enables him to control everyday objects simply by thinking about them. After drilling a hole into his head, surgeons implanted the chip a millimeter deep into his brain. Wafer-thin electrodes attached to the chip detect the electrical signals generated by his thoughts and relay them through wires into a computer. The brain signals are analyzed by the computer and translated into cursor movements. As well as operating a computer, software linked to other items in the room allows him to think his TV on and off and change channels.

Soaring Success
For her 1999 work, "100 Ideas in the Atmosphere," Canadian performance artist Marie-Suzanne Désilets launched 100 helium balloons from the rooftop of a Montreal shopping mall with self-addressed notecards and an invitation to reply.

ElasticMaN

DUBBED "MR ELASTIC," Moses Lanham can turn his feet around 180 degrees, completely backward, and then walk in the opposite direction!

Lanham puts his unique talent down to being born with extra ligaments and cartilage within the joints of his ankles, knees, and hips, which enable him to rotate his bones freely within the sockets of his joints.

Amazingly, he didn't realize he had this ability until he suffered a fall in gym class at the age of 14 and landed awkwardly. Jumping to his feet, he suddenly found that he could easily twist both of his feet around backward. Lanham, from Monroe, Michigan, has discovered that his son Trey also appears to have inherited the extra joint tissue. At 11, he could turn his feet backward just like his dad! "He can't walk backward yet," says Moses, "but he is learning."

Moses Lanham's body contains extra joint tissue that enables him to turn his feet backward. Moses can even walk backward too!

Moses enjoys putting his best foot backward, and often performs at local fund-raising events.

Wrist-breaker
That K.S. Raghavendra, from India, is capable of breaking 13 eggs in 30 seconds doesn't sound amazing in itself, except he doesn't break them by clenching his fist, but by bending his hand back over his wrist.

Hardy Eater
"Hungry" Charles Hardy, of Brooklyn, New York, describes himself as "the Michael Jordan of competitive eating." In 2001, he ate 23 hot dogs in 12 minutes, and also became Matzo Ball Eating world champion. But his talent has drawbacks. Hardy explains: "I found a place in Manhattan with all-you-can-eat sushi for $19.95. When the lady sees me coming, she hits the clock and gives me one and a half hours."

Button King
Dalton Stevens of Hartsville, South Carolina, has fixed an incredible 600,000 buttons to his Pontiac hearse. Another 60,000 buttons cover the coffin inside! Besides the hearse, he has shoes, musical instruments, and even a toilet covered with buttons.

Human Soap
A bar of soap that was said to have been made from body fat pumped from the Italian Prime Minister Silvio Berlusconi sold for almost $20,000 in 2005. Artist Gianni Motti said that he acquired the fat from a private Swiss clinic where Berlusconi reportedly underwent liposuction. Motti said the fat was "jelly-like and stunk horribly."

Heart Beat
Jeweler Didier Verhill, of Antwerp, Belgium, creates wedding rings engraved with the couple's heartbeat pattern taken from a cardiograph!

Ham Actors
Father and son, Olivier and Yohann Roussel, won one of Europe's most coveted prizes in 2005—the French Pig-squealing Championships. Dressed in pig outfits, the Roussels impressed the judges and spectators with squeals, grunts, and snuffles to represent the four key stages of a pig's life—birth, suckling, mating, and death under the knife.

Doctor, Doctor!

★ Dr. James T. Clack, of Wadley, Alabama, treated patients in the 1940s even though he was blind.

★ Allergist Dr. Edwin Dombrowski, of Stamford, Connecticut, had the automobile licence plate "AH-CHOO."

★ Dr. Anna Perkins, of Westerloo, New York, charged the same rates in 1993 that she had set in 1928: $4 for an office visit, $5 for a house call, and $25 to deliver a baby.

★ When Dr. William Price, of Llantrisant, south Wales, died in 1893, more than 6,000 tickets were sold for his public cremation, as specified in his will.

Between the Teeth
Lucky Rich, a street performer from Melbourne, Australia, had his teeth alloy-capped so that he can use them to extend the juggling and balancing act that he has performed all over the world. He can now support a woman swinging from a trapeze by holding the rope between his teeth.

HAIRS AND GRACES
Jo Jo "the Dog-faced Boy" was a circus performer in the 1880s. He suffered from a rare condition called hypertrichosis, which meant hair grew all over his face.

GOGGLE-EYED
Avelino Perez Matos, of Baracoa, Cuba, had the ability to dislocate each of his eyes out of their sockets whenever he chose.

HALF AND HALF
John "half-and-half man" Pecinovsky, from Bonair, Iowa, dressed himself in a different color on each side of his body, as well as shaving and not shaving!

MINI MARRIAGE
In 1863, "General Tom Thumb," or Charles Stratton, married Lavinia Warren. Lavinia was heralded as a miniature of perfect proportions, and the marriage was a major event in New York society.

[SMAL]L AND LARGE
Welsh giant George Auger and little person Tom Sordie both performed with the Barnum and Bailey Circus. Auger stood at 8 ft 6 in (2.6 m), while Sordie was a diminutive 2 ft 5 in (0.74 m).

SKINNY
Miss Agnes Schmidt, of Cincinnati, Ohio, pictured here in 1934, had rubber skin owing to a rare disease called Ehlers-Danlos Syndrome.

LOBSTER FEET
The fingers of this unidentified man from upstate western New York have mutated to look like lobster claws. This was the result of inbreeding.

INSEPARABLE TWINS
The "Tocci" twins were born with one body but two heads and four arms. The photo was taken in 1892 when they were 12 years old.

Looking Back

February 15th, 1890 **Frank Damek** stopped collecting stray cards from the street—he had at last made a full deck, after 20 years. **September 9, 1930** **Thurber Brockband** took nine hours to find a needle in a haystack. **May 2, 1802** **Timothy Dexter** published *A Pickle for the Knowing Ones*, a book that was full of intentionally misspelled words and without punctuation.

Species for Sale

A new species of rodent was discovered in 2005—for sale on a food stall in a market in Laos. The rock rat, or kha-nyou, was spotted by conservation biologist Robert Timmins who knew it was something he'd never seen before. The animal looks like a cross between a rat and a squirrel, but is not actually related to any other rodents.

Ledger Balancing

Balancing ledgers while balancing on ledges or deep-sea diving with a tax return are just some ways to perform Extreme Accounting. First established by Arnold Chiswick, the extreme sport incorporates everything involved in an accounting desk job with the thrill of sporting action.

Snake Diet

Neeranjan Bhaskar claims to have eaten more than 4,000 snakes, including deadly cobras. Bhaskar, who is a vegetarian otherwise, hunts for snakes every morning on the banks of the Ghagra River near his home in India. He first ate a snake at the age of seven.

Skin Horror

After being prescribed a common antibiotic to treat a routine sinus infection in 2003, Sarah Yeargain from San Diego, California, looked on in horror as her skin began peeling away in sheets. With Sarah's condition—caused by a severe allergic reaction to the drug—getting worse, more of her skin came off in her mother's hands as she was carried into a hospital. She eventually lost the skin from her entire body—including her internal organs and the membranes covering her mouth, throat, and eyes. Doctors gave her no chance of survival, but they covered her body in an artificial skin replacement and within a few days her own skin returned.

Dog Diver

When Dwane Folsom went scuba diving, his dog went too! Folsom, from Boynton Beach, Florida, designed the first scuba-diving outfit for dogs, including a lead-weighted jacket, a helmet, and a tube that allowed the animal to draw air from the human diver's tank. Folsom and his dog, named Shadow, regularly dived to depths of 13 ft (4 m).

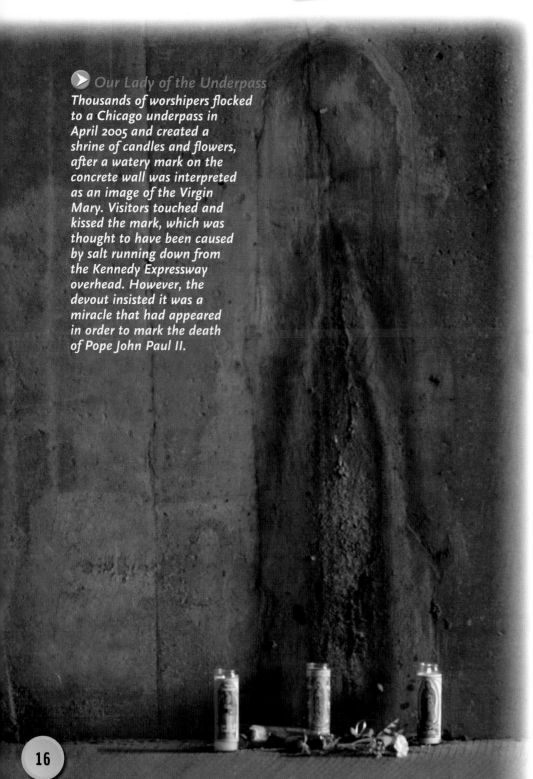

Our Lady of the Underpass

Thousands of worshipers flocked to a Chicago underpass in April 2005 and created a shrine of candles and flowers, after a watery mark on the concrete wall was interpreted as an image of the Virgin Mary. Visitors touched and kissed the mark, which was thought to have been caused by salt running down from the Kennedy Expressway overhead. However, the devout insisted it was a miracle that had appeared in order to mark the death of Pope John Paul II.

IN DEPTH
Live by the Sword

New Yorker Natasha Veruschka claims to be the world's only belly-dancing sword swallower, and defies a strict religious upbringing to risk her life for her passion.

When did you first become fascinated by swords?

❝ My British mother died when I was two. I don't remember my Siberian father—I was adopted into a strict Mennonite family in southern Ukraine. I wasn't allowed to hear music, or look in a mirror, or cut my hair. When I was four I saw a knife in a church—I was mesmerized. I remember putting the tip of it on my tongue to feel it. ❞

How did your act begin?

❝ I grew up in countries including India, Egypt, and Iran, and later took belly dancing lessons in New York.

I learned sword balancing, but one night I ended a performance by kissing the sword—I realized then that I wanted to be a sword swallower. The first time I did it, nine years ago, it felt like home—it made me complete. ❞

What kinds of swords do you swallow?

❝ The longest is 27½ inches—which is a lot because I am only 5 ft 4 in tall and weigh just over 100 lb. I have 25 different swords—including a Sai sword, which is an eight-sided Japanese war weapon. I can swallow up to 13 swords at once. ❞

Which is the most dangerous?

❝ The neon sword, which is filled with poisonous gas and is so fragile that your stomach muscles can shatter it inside you. It is electric and heats up—one time, it started to burn and adhere to my insides. Since 1942, six people have died swallowing one. ❞

Have you ever cut yourself on a sword?

❝ Once I nearly died—I lost 53 per cent of my blood. I had three swords inside me and a man pushed me. The blades scissored and cut my lower esophagus. After the show, I was vomiting blood everywhere and even had a near-death experience. They told me at the hospital that I would be in the morgue by the following morning. I was back swallowing swords within a month. ❞

Where does the sword go?

❝ To the bottom of the stomach. I can swallow a chocolate cherry, put a sword down and bring it back up. You have to overcome much more than a gag reflex—the sword has to go past two muscle sphincters as well, on its way past the lungs and heart. ❞

Do you have any special techniques?

❝ I say a prayer before every performance, and use yoga to go into 'a zone.' I use no lubricant, no special tubes. You need a lot of upper body strength—the swords weigh close to 12½ lb when I swallow them all at once—and a lot of lung capacity. It's not magic. I have been X-rayed and you can see the sword in me. The neon one glows through my body for all to see. ❞

What drives you—and how long will you do this?

❝ My family have shunned me for what I do. To them, I am dead. I think this all stems from an 'I'll show you' attitude. As for how long, I won't be happy until I'm the oldest female belly-dancing sword swallower in the world! ❞

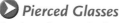
Free Pig

In an unusual bid to boost sales in 2005, an entrepreneurial British housing developer offered a free gift of a live pig to anyone who bought a property from him. Jeremy Paxton, who is based in Gloucestershire, England, promised that the rare breed Gloucester Old Spot pigs would be fully house-trained before delivery.

Giant Rodent

For a 2004 art festival, Dutchman Florentun Hofman built a sculpture of a beaver 100 ft (31 m) long and 25 ft (8 m) high, using just wood and reeds. The year before, he made a 37-ft (11-m) high rabbit.

▶ Pierced Glasses

An American artist has had permanent glasses pierced through the bridge of his nose. Twenty-three-year-old James Sooy, from Dallas, Texas, came up with the eye-catching invention to stop his spectacles from constantly slipping down his nose. The piercing features magnets, so that he can take the glasses off when he bathes and sleeps.

Nose Grown

Madina Yusuf had her face reconstructed by growing a new nose on her arm. The Nigerian woman was severely disfigured by a flesh-eating disease that left her without a nose and with very little mouth. But, in 2001, she flew to Aberdeen, Scotland, where Dr. Peter Ayliffe grafted her new nose from extra skin grown on her arm, plus bone and cartilage that had been taken from her right rib.

Balloon Sculpture

U.S. balloon sculptor Larry Moss used more than 40,000 balloons to construct a model of two football players at Mol, Belgium, in 2000. Each player was 40 ft (12 m) tall.

The Smell of Italy!

In 2003, Ducio Cresci, of Florence, Italy, created bathroom products—including soap, lotion, and bubble bath—that smelled just like pizza!

◀ Superhuman Suit

Japanese scientists have designed a robot suit that gives you superhuman strength. People wearing the HAL (Hybrid Assistive Limb) exoskeleton have been able to carry 88 lb (40 kg) more than they could normally. The equipment reads nerve signals sent from the brain to muscles in the wearer's arms or legs. Motors then start up to support the limbs as the wearer moves. It is hoped that the suit could help disabled people to walk.

Tiny Tackler

The ace defence tackler on the football team at Flint Southwestern Academy High School, Michigan, was only 3 ft (0.9 m) tall, having been left with no legs after a 1994 railroad accident. Willie McQueen earned his place on the team by courage and tenacity. He didn't play in a wheelchair or wear prostheses, but scooted around to create havoc in the opposing backfield.

SWISS ENGINEERS have designed a car that reacts to your mood. The **Rinspeed Senso** can introduce **relaxing smells** and will even **shake** the seat to wake you up if it thinks you've dozed off at the wheel.

Garbage Tour

In Chicago in 2005, people were paying $7 to see some of the city's less desirable spots on a three-hour bus tour of garbage sites, landfills, and smelly sludge sewage fields. The excursion showed residents and visitors what happens to garbage once it leaves their trash cans.

Astral Grooming

Astronauts in space shave using razors equipped with tiny vacuum cleaners inside!

Mini Cows
In a bid to combat his country's serious milk shortage of 1987, Fidel Castro urged his scientists to create a breed of mini cows. Castro wanted the most productive cows cloned and shrunk to the size of dogs so that families could keep one inside their apartments. There, the cows would feed on grass grown under fluorescent lights.

Peculiar Pastimes
In Rieti, Italy, there is an annual washtub race in which contestants race wooden washtubs along a course 875 yds (800 m) long.

Extreme Carving
In Port Elgin, Ontario, Canada, there is an annual pumpkin festival that includes such events as underwater pumpkin carving.

▶ Wrappers Reborn
Finnish artist Virpi Vesanen-Laukkanen exhibited this dress, in St. Petersburg, Russia, made entirely of candy wrappers. The artist said that her creation reminded her of sweets eaten during long journeys.

Busse Load
When the Busse family marked the 150th anniversary of the arrival of their ancestors in the U.S.A. from Germany, it was no ordinary reunion: 2,369 family members turned up at Grayslake, Illinois, in 1998, some from as far away as Africa.

◀ Huge Halloween
Belgian artist Michel Dircken sits in his carving, created during a competition for the fastest carving of a jack o'lantern in October 2005. The pumpkin weighed 637 lb (289 kg) and measured 131 in (333 cm) around.

Space Oddity
Canadian performance artist Julie Andrée T. sought to redefine space by walking blindfold in a confined space for six hours, marking the walls and singing a children's song.

Competitive Kite-flying
Kite fighting is common at the spring Festival of Basant in Lahore, Pakistan. Skilled kite-flyers from all around the country use bladed and chemical-lined strings to bring down or capture their opponents' kites.

Birth Art
As part of an exhibition in a German art gallery, a woman gave birth in front of dozens of spectators. Ramune Gele had the baby girl, named Audra, in 2005, at the DNA gallery in Berlin. The father, Winfried Witt, called the experience "an existential work of art."

Two Noses
Bill Durks was born in 1913 with two noses, each with a single nostril. Between the bridges of his noses, he painted a third eye, over what may have been a vestigial eye socket, and became known in U.S. sideshows as "The Man with Three Eyes." He married Milly Durks, "The Alligator-skinned Woman From New Jersey."

FyRe EaTeR

EATING FIRE, swallowing swords, juggling machetes, hammering nails up his own nose—they're all in a day's work for the Amazing Blazing Tyler Fyre!

Fyre (real name Tyler Fleet), born in Georgia, was unique even as a kid, when he found that he could squirt milk, water, and even spaghetti and meatballs out of his nose. He learned trapeze, juggling, balancing, the high wire, and fire-eating, before progressing to a routine as a Human Blockhead. In ten years, Fyre, who also eats glass, razor blades, live crickets, and lit cigarettes, and has been known to pound a nail through a hole in his tongue, has done more than 7,500 live shows, sometimes performing 15 a day. He admits: "It's grueling on the body. At the Coney Island Circus Sideshow I was the Human Blockhead, the sword swallower, I ate fire, and I did the inverted escape act, cranked up by my ankles until my head was 6 ft (1.8 m) above the stage."

Tyler learned his fire-eating from a fellow student while training to be a circus performer. Of all his sideshow skills, it remains his first love.

Tyler used to hammer a nail through the hole in his tongue. He still enjoys putting toothpicks in it.

In a daring escapology routine, Tyler is tied in a straitjacket and hung upside down by his ankles 6 ft (1.8 m) above the stage.

When it comes to swallowing swords, Tyler's act puts him at the cutting edge of show business.

Killer Tree

In 1860, nearly 200 years after his death, the Rhode Island Historical Society exhumed the body of Roger Williams—only to find that he had been eaten by an apple tree! The coffin was empty apart from the invading tree roots. A large root curved where his head should have been and entered the chest cavity before growing down the spine. It then branched at the two legs and upturned into feet.

Ice Sculptor

Richard Bubin, from Wilkins, Pennsylvania, has been sculpting ice for over 20 years and once carved 61 blocks in under 4½ hours. For Pittsburgh's First Night celebration in January 2005, he turned ten giant blocks of ice into a sculpture of the Roberto Clemente Bridge.

Jumbo Junk

British artist Anthony Heywood made a full-size elephant sculpture in 2004 entirely from household junk, including TV sets, heaters, fans, radios, and a toilet.

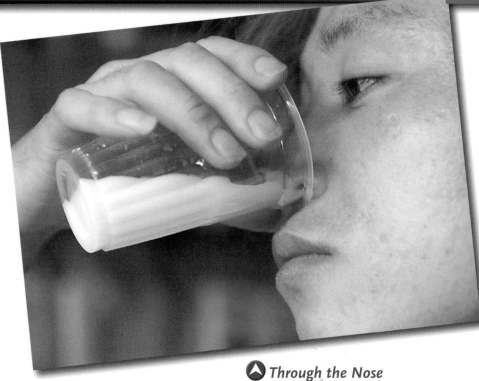

Stair Ride

In the 2005 urban Down the Hill bike race, held in the town of Taxco, Mexico, competitors rode their mountain bikes through a house! They went in through a door, down a flight of stairs and exited through another door. They also sped through narrow alleys and jumped heights of 13 ft (4 m) on the 2-mi (3.2-km) course.

▲ Through the Nose

Jin Guolong, from China, can drink through his nose—he consumes both milk and alcohol using this method.

Legged It!

A man testing an artificial leg worth $17,000 ran off without paying the bill. The theft occurred after the man called in to collect a prosthetic from a specialist in Des Moines, Iowa, in 2005, and was allowed to take it away for a couple of hours to ensure that it fitted him properly.

Chicken Protest

Ottawa performance artist Rob Thompson caged a man and a woman in 1997 to protest about the conditions of commercially bred chickens. Eric Wolf and Pam Meldrum spent a week together in the small wooden cage to make the point. Their drinking water came from a dripping hose and they ate vegetarian mash.

Love Birds

During the Middle Ages, people in Europe are said to have believed that birds chose their mates every year on Valentine's Day!

X-ray Eyes

A teenage Russian girl appears to have X-ray vision, which enables her to see inside human bodies. Natalia Demkina has baffled scientists across the world by describing the insides of bodies in detail and using her talent to correctly diagnose the medical conditions of complete strangers. She says that she possesses dual vision when looking at others, but that she can't see inside her own body.

Natalia can switch from normal to X-ray vision by focusing on a person for two minutes.

Pet Pillows

In 2005, Nevada taxidermist Jeanette Hall offered to make fur pillows from dead pets. Each Pet Pillow was handmade for prices ranging from $65 for a cat to $150 for a horse. Hall described the idea as a "unique way of keeping your pets close to you even after they pass away."

Shopping Break

Tired shoppers in Minnesota's Mall of America can rest their weary legs for 70 cents a minute. In the Bloomington shopping center there is a store called MinneNAPolis aimed at bored spouses of shoppers and also at travelers, who need a nap after a lengthy flight, but aren't staying long enough to book a hotel.

Circus Sideshow

★ Prince Randian, known as "The Living Torso," had no arms or legs. However, he amazingly learned to roll, light, and smoke a cigarette by moving his mouth.

★ Myrtle Corbin, the four-legged woman from Texas, had a malformed conjoined twin, which resulted in Myrtle having two pairs of legs. She used to gallop across the stage like a horse.

★ Edward Mordrake was born a conjoined twin, and had another face on the reverse of his—that of a beautiful girl whose eyes used to follow you around the room.

Pavement Picasso

Ben Wilson roams the streets of London, England, looking for used chewing gum, which he turns into works of art. He burns the gum with a blowtorch, adds a clear enamel as a base, then colors in acrylic enamels, and finishes with a coat of varnish. His gum gallery includes human portraits, animals, and buildings.

Cricket Lover

Danny Capps of Madison, Wisconsin, spits dead crickets from his mouth over distances of up to 30 ft (9 m). Capps, who has been fascinated by insects since he was a small boy, says that dead crickets have no flavor.

Winter Woollies

In 2001, a group of volunteers in Tasmania, Australia, knitted turtleneck sweaters for a colony of rare Australian penguins to protect the birds against oil spills!

Robot Riders

In 2005, Qatar, in the Middle East, staged a spectacular camel race using robot jockeys. Seven robots were placed on top of seven camels at Al Shahaniyya racecourse, near the country's capital Doha, after there had been widespread protests about the use of children as jockeys in the popular sport.

▲ Pretty as a Picture

A participant in the 13th International Tattoo Convention, held in Frankfurt, Germany, in 2005, sports a tattoo on the back of his head.

Sensitive Shirt

Italian designer Francesca Rosella has come up with the perfect gift for people involved in long-distance relationships—a hugging T-shirt. Fitted with sensors, the T-shirt simulates the missing partner's caress by recreating breath, touch, and heartbeat based on information transmitted via their cell phone.

Time Capsule

At the 1957 Tulsarama Festival in Tulsa, Oklahoma, a brand-new Chrysler car was buried in a time capsule, to be unearthed in 2007. People were asked to guess Tulsa's population in 2007. The family of Raymond Humbertson ended up winning what had become a rusted hunk of metal.

CUTLERY ART
A figure made from ordinary knives, forks, and spoons.

ONE OF RIPLEY'S BIGGEST, this museum in Mexico City can be found in an eye-catching replica medieval castle. Open since 1992, it features a full-size humpback whale skeleton and a giant solid jade Buddha with 1,000 hands.

TOAST ART
The *Mona Lisa* created in a toaster from 64 pieces of white bread.

THEATER MASK
A rare Indonesian Topeng mask of a bulging-eyed demon.

DON'T MISS!

► Painting on a rice grain
► Flag flown in space aboard *Apollo 7*
► Human faces painted on a human hair
► Spiked collar-torture device
► Leo Sewell junk art figures
► Collection of metal objects removed from a human stomach
► Egyptian mummified head
► Smallest working camera

CROCODILE NECKLACE
This necklace from New Guinea is made from crocodile teeth, and was worn for luck.

LINCOLN LOG CABIN
Made from 18,000 Lincoln pennies, this replica of Abraham Lincoln's place of birth weighs 200 lb (90 kg).

TONGUE DEXTERITY
Can you roll or fold your tongue? One in 1,000 can. Find out if you can with this interactive display inside the museum.

GATEKEEPER'S MASK
An Indian mask that is hung on gates and entrances to ward off evil spirits.

WHALE SKELETON
This humpback whale was the first ever to be put on public display in New York City in the 1840s.

ROOT CARVING
The material used to create this traditional Chinese carving is a tree root.

Pregnant Boy

When seven-year-old Alamjan Nematilaev's tummy began to bulge, his parents thought he had rickets, a common childhood disease in his native Kazakhstan. But, in 2003, a concerned schoolteacher took him to hospital, where doctors removed a 4-lb (1.8-kg) baby boy from Alamjan's stomach! Alamjan had been born with the fetus of his twin brother growing inside him. For seven years it had lived like a parasite, growing a head, a body, hair, and nails. Doctors were able to save Alamjan but not the 8-in (20-cm) fetus.

Medical Marvels

★ When teenager Doug Pritchard, of Lenoir, North Carolina, went to his doctor in 1978 with a sore foot, a tooth was found growing in the bottom of his instep!

★ Jens Jenson, of Denmark, fell into a pile of spiky barberries in 1990 and had to visit his doctor 248 times to have a total of 32,131 thorns removed from his punctured body.

★ After Peter Morris from Kingswinford, England, lost his thumb in a 1993 accident, doctors replaced it with his big toe.

★ Trampled by a bull in 1993, Jim McManus, of Calgary, Canada, had his left ear reattached by doctors—aided by 75 leeches to control the bleeding.

In Fond Memory
Swedish artist and sculptor Lars Widenfalk has created a violin with a difference. He sculpted the working instrument from the tombstone of his late grandfather, Gustav. The violin's fingerboard, pegs, tailpiece, and chin rest are all made of ebony, and by lining the interior with real gold, it produces the finest possible tone. The instrument is considered to be worth in the region of $1.7 million.

Small Wonder
Ma Chaoqin from China was 22 years old in this photo, but still looked like a baby. She suffers from a disease called Rachitic, or rickets, and as a result failed to grow at a normal rate.

Wall Eater

In 2005, Emily Katrencik ate through the wall of her Brooklyn gallery until she could put her head through it—all in the name of art. She said: "The wall has a mild flavor. The texture is more prominent than the taste—it's chalky with tiny sharp pieces in it." Visitors could eat bread made with minerals extracted from the wall.

Frog Birth

A woman from Iran was reported to have given birth to a gray frog-like creature in 2004. It apparently grew from a larva that had entered the woman as she swam in a dirty pool. A doctor described the creature as resembling a frog in appearance, particularly the shape of the fingers, and the size and shape of the tongue.

Talon Contest

Louise Hollis of Compton, California, has let her toenails grow to a staggering 6 in (15 cm) long. She has to wear open-toed shoes with at least 3-in (7.6-cm) soles to stop her nails dragging along the ground, and she needs 2½ bottles of nail polish to paint the nails on both her hands and feet.

Pan Christ

As Juan Pastrano, of Prairie Lea, Texas, was hanging up his frying pan after washing it in 2005, he spotted an uncanny image where the anti-stick coating on the pan had worn thin. There before him was the face of Jesus Christ in a crown of thorns. He promptly sealed the pan in a plastic bag to protect the image from curious visitors.

HEaRiNG CoLoRS

COLOR-BLIND art student Neil Harbisson wears a special device that enables him to "hear" colors.

Neil now paints in vibrant colors.

Neil, from Spain, uses a device called the Eye-Borg, that was invented by Adam Montandon, a digital multimedia expert from Plymouth, England. It works by converting light waves into sounds, and consists of a digital camera and a backpack that contains the computer and headset for Neil to listen to the colors. A low-pitched sound indicates reds, a high-pitched sound indicates violet, while shades of blue and green fall somewhere in between.

Now Neil, who takes off the invention only when he sleeps, is able to buy clothes that he "likes the sound of." He can also order his favorite foods, whereas previously he struggled to differentiate between apple juice and orange juice.

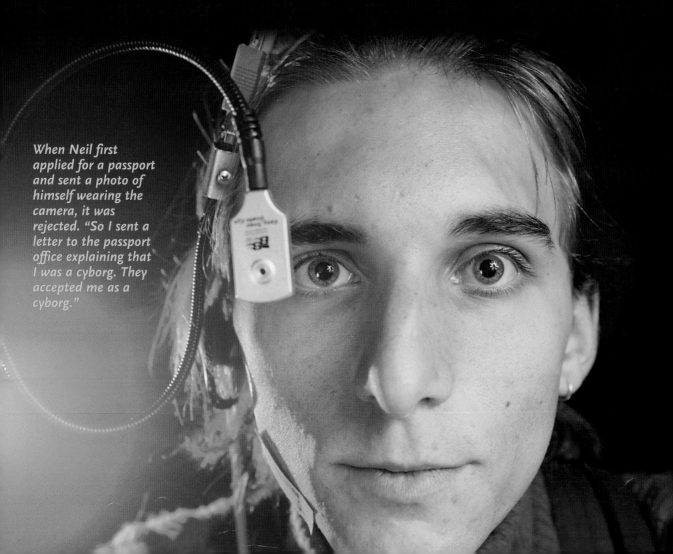

When Neil first applied for a passport and sent a photo of himself wearing the camera, it was rejected. "So I sent a letter to the passport office explaining that I was a cyborg. They accepted me as a cyborg."

Two Hearts

A boy in Tbilisi, Georgia, was born with two hearts. In 2004, doctors discovered that one-year-old Goga Diasamidze had been born with a second perfectly functioning heart near his stomach.

⏷ Stinger Swallow

For more than 20 years a village in Dorset, England has hosted the World Stinging Nettle Eating Championships. Each brave entrant must tear the leaves from stalks of stinging nettles and swallow them. Rules are strict, the bare stalks are measured and the competitor who has stripped the longest nettles, and eaten all the stinging leaves, is declared the winner. The record length is 76 ft (23 m) of painfully chewed nettles.

Miracle Heart

Nikolai Mikhalnichuk leads a healthy life even though his heart stopped beating several years ago. He suffered a heart attack when his wife said she was leaving him, but doctors in Saratov, Russia, found that although his heart has stopped, its blood vessels are able to keep on pumping blood around his body.

Omelette Surprise

When Ursula Beckley of Long Island, New York, was preparing an omelette in 1989, she cracked open an egg—only to see a 6-in (15-cm) black snake slither out. She sued her local supermarket for $3.6 million on the grounds that she was so traumatized by the incident that she could never look at an egg again.

Snail Trail

In Januray 2005, Chilean artist Paola Podesta promoted her new exhibition by gluing 2,000 plastic snails to a Santiago church. The snail trail led from the Church of Santo Expedito to the nearby Codar art gallery.

Snowball Flag

In 1998, Vasili Mochanou, of Ottawa, Ontario, created a replica of the Canadian Flag using 27,000 snowballs!

Steve Relles makes a living by scooping up **dog poop**! The *Delmar Dog Butler*, as he calls himself, has over **100 clients** in NEW YORK STATE who pay **$10** each for a **weekly clean** of their yard.

Snake Man

For more than 50 years, Bill Haast injected himself with deadly snake venom. He built up such powerful antibodies in his system that his blood was used as a snakebite antidote. Haast, who ran a Florida serpentarium, began in 1948 with tiny amounts of rattlesnake venom and built up the dosage until, by the time he was 90, he was injecting himself once a week with venom from 32 species. Although he was bitten more than 180 times by snakes from which a few drops of venom could kill any ordinary human, Haast managed to survive every single time.

Head Reattached

Marcos Parra must be one of the luckiest guys alive. He survived a horrific car accident in 2002, in which his head was technically severed from the rest of his body. His skull was torn from his cervical spine, leaving his head detached from his neck. Only skin and his spinal cord kept the two body parts connected. Amazingly, however, surgeons in Phoenix, Arizona, managed to reattach his head. The bones were pulled into the right position by two screws placed at the back of his neck, enabling Parra to live.

Last Ride of your Life!

Gordon Fitch took his passion for motorcycles to a new level when he started his Blackhawk Hearse business. For a fitting and dignified last ride, bikers can have their coffins drawn by a Harley Davidson motorcycle.

Bushy Brows

In 2004, Frank Ames of Saranac, New York State, had his eyebrow hair measured at an incredible 3.1 in (7.8 cm). Ames said "I don't know why it grows like that. It just always has."

Hot Stuff

New Mexico State University has developed a special Halloween chili pepper, a miniature ornamental specimen that changes from black to orange. However, Paul Bosland, head of the university's chili-breeding program, warns that these hot peppers are actually too hot to eat.

Turtle Recall

In 2005, a Chinese man pretended to be a hunchback in order to smuggle his pet turtle onto a plane. The elderly man strapped the turtle, which was 8 in (20 cm) in diameter, to his back before boarding a flight to Chongqing, but after getting through security, he was stopped by a guard who thought his hump looked strange.

Fish Bones

Chinese artist Liu Huirong recreates famous works of art in fish bones! She took two years and used more than 100,000 fish bones to complete a copy of "Spring's Back," a 300-year-old painting by Yuan Jiang. She has been making fish-bone pictures for more than 20 years. Every day she collects fish bones from roadside garbage bins and degreases, marinates, and chemically treats them before sticking them onto canvas.

Branching Out

For more than 25 years, performance artist David "The Bushman" Johnson has been alarming people on Fisherman's Wharf, San Francisco, by jumping out from behind branches as they pass by. He has been arrested over 1,000 times as a result of people not getting the joke.

Bone Sculpture

In 2001, U.S. artist Sarah Perry created "Beast of Burden," a 9-ft (2.7-m) rocketship made from horse and cattle bones! She has created other sculptures from hundreds of tiny rodent bones, which she has painstakingly extracted from owl pellets. She also makes art using junk that has been discarded in the Nevada Desert and once made a 700-lb (318-kg) gorilla from old rubber truck-tires.

Speak with Forked Tongue
A multi-pierced and tattooed young man, who wanted to be known only as "Ian," had his tongue split in May 2003 to resemble that of a snake. He also installed fang caps on his teeth.

Raw Talent

Gabriela Rivera horrified visitors to an art gallery in Santiago, Chile, in 2005, by showing a video of herself with her face covered in raw meat. She said it showed the relationship people have with themselves each day when they look in the mirror.

In 2001, an **insurance company** in Great Britain offered a "**Spooksafe**" policy for *death, injury, or damage* caused by a **ghost** or **poltergeist**.

Hair Force

Indian police have been trying to improve their public image by paying officers to grow mustaches. In 2004, chiefs in Madhya Pradesh announced a monthly mustache bonus of 30 rupees (about 50 cents) after research showed that officers with smart facial hair were taken more seriously. Mustaches are a sign of authority in India.

Over Your Head
Shanghai, in China, saw the premiere of what was billed as the first acrobatic ballet—a combination of Western dance and ancient Chinese acrobatics. In this scene from "Swan Lake the Acrobatic," a ballerina balanced on her toes on the head of a male dancer.

In a Twist

Los Angeles contortionist Daniel Browning Smith is otherwise known as The Rubberboy—he is so flexible he can cram his whole body into a box the size of a microwave oven.

When did you first discover your flexibility?

"I was four years old when I jumped off my bunk bed and landed in a perfect saddle split. I showed my father and he went to the library and brought me home pictures of contortionists—I tried to copy them, and I could. As a kid playing hide and seek I could hide in the sock drawer!"

How did you turn that into a career?

"When I was 18, the circus came through the town where I grew up in Mississippi. I told my family I was joining it and would be back in three weeks—that was eight years ago."

Does it hurt?

"I practice a stretch until just before it becomes painful, then hold it a bit until it feels normal, then stretch a bit further. The connective tissue between my bones is different genetically, inherited from both sides of my family. My father's father was in the military and it helped him to dislocate his hips when it was time to march. The stretches I do enhance that for me."

What exactly can you do?

"I believe I am the most flexible person alive. Most contortionists can only bend one way—I can bend so far backwards the top of my head touches the seat of my pants, and so far forward I can kiss my own behind! I can also disconnect both arms, both legs, and turn my torso 180 degrees."

What is your favorite stunt?

"De-Escape—it is the complete opposite of Houdini's straitjacket routine. I have to dislocate my arms and squeeze into a locked straitjacket, then chain myself up with my mouth and flip myself into a box."

What else can you do?

"I can make my ribcage go up and my abdomen go down so you can see my heart beating through my skin! And I can get into a box about the size of a microwave. I get my shins in first, because I can't bend them, then my back, then my head and arms fill the holes. I have to slow down my breathing because my arms and legs put pressure on my lungs."

Have you ever got stuck?

"I can get through an unstrung tennis racquet or a toilet seat, but once a toilet seat got stuck around my torso with my thigh in the hole as well. I was home alone, and had to crawl into the kitchen and get a bottle of vegetable oil and pour it all over me. The seat finally came off—I just made a huge mess."

Are you working on future stunts?

"I'm trying to turn my head 180 degrees. I can get to about 175 degrees already. It's the only thing I've tried that's made me gasp—it's weird looking down and seeing your own butt!"

Rock Around the Clock

Suresh Joachim, from Mississauga, Ontario, spent 3 days 3 hours 3 minutes 3 seconds rocking in a rocking chair nonstop in August 2005. In the course of his challenge at the Hilton Garden Inn, Toronto, Ontario, he ate just one plain white roll, some noodle soup, three hard-boiled eggs, and one and a half potatoes. He also drank water and energy drinks, but not enough so that he would have to go to the bathroom. His greatest fear was falling asleep because of the continuous rocking back and forth.

Chomping Champ

Australian "Bushtucker Freddy" devours a locust during the 2005 Bug Eating Championships. He went on to win the competition that involved challengers from all over the world eating a variety of creepy crawlies, such as crickets, mealworms, hornets, and locusts.

Blood Stains

Mexican artist Teresa Margolles staged a 2005 exhibition in Metz, France, featuring clothing stained with human blood. She worked in a morgue for ten years and her display consisted of clothes worn by corpses.

> Heads turn when **Paul Miller,** from **Alta Loma,** California, walks down the street. That's because his **mustache** is **10 ft (3 m)** long! It takes him *an hour* to groom it each day.

Hair Wear

Nina Sparre, of Vamhuf, Sweden, practices the art of Haarkulla, or "Hair Farming," creating art and clothing out of human hair!

Living Billboard

Forty models lived in a 3-D billboard on the side of a building for two days in July 2005, creating New York City's first-ever live billboard. They were advertising a new fragrance from Calvin Klein. The models were told to create an illusion of a big party, 24 hours a day.

Car Polish

You can't miss Yvonne Millner when she drives down the streets of Hopkins, South Carolina—hers is the car decorated in nail polish. She started by painting on a smiling face, but now she has designs and slogans all over her car, including a palm tree and the words "Hang Loose." She spends three to four hours a day on the creation and has used over 100 bottles of nail polish.

Hidden Monkeys

When Californian Robert Cusack was asked if he had anything to declare on arrival at Los Angeles Airport in 2002, customs officers could hardly have expected what they would find. They discovered a pair of pygmy monkeys in his pants and a bird of paradise in his suitcase. Cusack was subsequently sentenced to 57 days in jail for smuggling the monkeys, as well as four exotic birds, and 50 rare orchids into the U.S.A. from Thailand.

Fancy Dress

The first prize in the youth division of the July 4 Parade in Haines, Oregon, in 2005, went to three children dressed as dung beetles! Wearing tubes covered by garbage bags, they pushed huge rubber balls coated in sand, dirt, and dead grass.

Ambidextrous Bilinguist

In 2004, Amanullah, a 53-year-old man from India, learned to write different sentences simultaneously with both hands. Most amazing of all, he could write one sentence in English, and the other in Tamil.

Pulling Power

The Great Nippulini can tow a car from the piercings attached to his nipples, as well as lift a phenomenal 55 lb (25 kg).

Holy Shower

In 2005, Jeffrey Rigo of Pittsburgh, Pennsylvania, sold a water stain on his bathroom wall for nearly $2,000 because he thought that it bore a resemblance to Jesus. Following the publicity for the "Shower Jesus," Rigo had requests from people who wanted to pray in his bathtub.

Emergency Repairs

Jonas Scott, from Salt Lake City, Utah, was left with no esophagus after industrial cleaning fluid at his workplace ate away his insides in 1988. With no stomach, he had to be fed intravenously. He went three years without eating solids until surgeons connected the remaining 7 ft (2.1 m) of his small intestine directly to the base of his throat so that he could eat almost normally again.

Great Balls of Fire!
Stonehenge in Wiltshire, England, was the location for a massive synchronized fire-eating spectacular. Seventy fire-eaters came together to create a landscape of flames at the event in September 2004.

Index

A

accounting, extreme 16, *16*
acrobatic ballet 30, *30*
airplanes, smuggled animals 29, 33
Amanullah (Ind) 33
ambushes, performance art 30
Ames, Frank (U.S.A.) 29
armless and legless man 23
art
    blood-stained clothes 32
    fish-bone pictures 30
    from human hair 32
    see also paintings; performance art; sculpture
astronauts, shaving 18
Auger, George (U.K.) 15, *15*
Ayliffe, Dr. Peter (U.K.) 18

B

ballet, acrobatic 30, *30*
balloons
    performance art 10
    sculpture from 18
bathroom products, pizza-smelling 18
beads, enormous collection of 8
beards
    bearded lady 8
    shaving in space 18
Beatles memorabilia, toilet paper 8, *8*
beaver, giant sculpture of 18
Beckley, Ursula (U.S.A.) 28
belly dancing, and sword swallowing (U.S.A.) 17, *17*
Berlusconi, Silvio (Ita) 12
Bhaskar, Neeranjan (Ind) 16
bicycles, mountain bike race through house 22
billboard, living 32
birds, choosing mates 22
birth
    as performance art 19
    woman gives birth to frog 26
blind doctor 12
blindfold performance art 19
blood-stained clothes, as art 32
bones
    fish-bone pictures 30
    sculpture 30
book, intentional misspellings 15
Bosland, Paul (U.S.A.) 29
brain, remote control implant 10
bread
    edible human bodies 6, *6–7*
    Mona Lisa made from toast 24, *24*
Brockband, Thurber (U.S.A.) 15
Brokl, Bettye Jane (U.S.A.) 10

Bubin, Richard (U.S.A.) 22
building, covered in love letters 10
"Bushtucker Freddy" (Aus) 32, *32*
Busse family (U.S.A.) 19
buttons, coffin covered in 12, *12*

C

California Institute of Abnormalarts (U.S.A.) 8
camel race, robot jockeys 23
candy wrappers, dress made of 19, *19*
Capps, Danny (U.S.A.) 23
cards *see* playing cards
cars
    buried in time capsule 23
    identifying insect splats on 9
    nail polish decoration 32
    personalized licence plates 12
    pulling with nipples 33, *33*
    reacting to your mood 18
carvings, tree root 25
Castro, Fidel (Cub) 19
cat, two-faced kitten 9
chewing gum art 23
Chicago (U.S.A.), tour of garbage sites 18
chickens, performance art protest 22
chilis, too hot to eat 29
Chiswick, Arnold 16, *16*
church, plastic snails glued to 28
circus memorabilia 8
Clack, Dr. James T. (U.S.A.) 12
clothes
    blood-stained clothes as art 32
    candy-wrapper dress 19, *19*
    from human hair 32
    hugging T-shirts 23
    knitting sweaters for penguins 23
coffins
    covered in buttons 12, *12*
    motorcycle hearse 29, *29*
    tree roots in 22
coins, Lincoln birthplace replica made of pennies 25
colors, "hearing" 27, *27*
contortionists
    flexible feet 11, *11*
    flexible wrists 12, *12*
    The Rubberboy (U.S.A.) 31, *31*
Corbin, Myrtle (U.S.A.) 23
cows, miniature 19
cremation
    paintings with ashes 10
    in public 12
Cresci, Ducio (Ita) 18
Crew, Carl (U.S.A.) 8
crickets, spitting dead 23
crocodiles, tooth necklace 24
Cusack, Robert (U.S.A.) 33
cutlery sculpture 24
Cwayita, Nhlahla (S.A.) 8
cyborgs 27, *27*

D

Damek, Frank (U.S.A.) 15, *15*
Désilets, Marie-Suzanne (Can) 10
Dexter, Timothy (U.S.A.) 15
Diasamidze, Goga (Geo) 28
Dircken, Michel (Bel) 19, *19*
diving, scuba-diving dog 16
doctors
    blind 12
    frozen fees 12
    personalized number plates 12
dogs
    dog-poop cleaner 28
    scuba diving 16
Dombrowski, Dr. Edwin (U.S.A.) 12
dress, candy-wrapper 19, *19*
dung
    dog-poop cleaner 28
    dung beetle fancy dress 33
    sculpture 9
Durks, Bill and Milly (U.S.A.) 19

E

ear, severed ear reattached 26
eggs
    breaking with hand bent backwards 12, *12*
    snake found in 28
elephant, junk sculpture 22
escapology, from straitjacket 20, 21
Evans, Megan (Can) 9
extreme sports
    accounting 16, *16*
    underwater pumpkin carving 19
eyebrows, lengthy 29
eyes
    dislocating out of sockets 14, *14*
    X-ray vision 22, *22*

F

faces
    covered in hair 14, *14*
    covered in raw meat 30
    two-faced kitten 9
    two-faced man 23
family reunion, enormous 19
fancy dress, dung beetle 33
fat, soap made from human 12
feet
    amputated 9
    extra toes 10, *10*
    like lobster claws 15, *15*
    thumb replaced with big toe 26
    tooth growing in 26
    walking with heels twisted backwards 11, *11*
Ferguson, Robert (U.S.A.) 8
fighting, with kites 19
fingers, extra 10, *10*
fire, marriage proposal 9, *9*
fire-eating 20–21, *20–21*
    synchronized demonstration 33
fish-bone pictures 30

Fitch, Gordon (U.S.A.) 29, *29*
flag, snowball replica 29
Folsom, Dwayne (U.S.A.) 16
food and drink
    intravenous feeding 33
    nettles, eating 28, *28–29*
    speed eating 12
    unusual food items
        human bodies made from bread 6, *6–7*
        locusts 32, *32*
        snakes 16
        wall 26
football, legless player 18
forged signatures 9
frog, woman gives birth to 26
frying pan, image of Jesus Christ on 26
funerals
    motorcycle hearse 29, *29*
    public cremation 12
fur, dead-pet pillows 23
Fyre (Tyler Fleet) (U.S.A.) 20–21, *20–21*

G

garbage sites, tour of 18
Gele, Ramune (Ger) 19
gerbil, installation art 10
ghosts, insurance against 30
giant, circus act 15, *15*
glasses, attached to nose piercing 18, *18*
Grannis, Todd (U.S.A.) 9, *9*
grave, tree roots in coffin 22

H

Haast, Bill (U.S.A.) 28
hair
    art and clothing from human hair 32
    growing all over face 14, *14*
    letters carved on 8
    long eyebrows 29
    see also beards; mustaches
Hall, Jeanette (U.S.A.) 23
hands
    extra fingers 10, *10*
    like lobster claws 15, *15*
    thumb replaced with big toe 26
Harbisson, Neil (Spa) 27, *27*
Hardy, Charles "Hungry" (U.S.A.) 12
haystack, finding needle in 15
head
    almost severed from body 29
    tattoos on back of 23, *23*
    see also faces
"hearing" colors 27, *27*
hearses
    covered in buttons 12
    motorcycle 29, *29*
heart
    life after heartbeat stopped 29
    second heart 28
heartbeats, engraved on rings 12
helium balloons, as art 10

Heywood, Anthony (U.K.) 22
Hofman, Florentun (Net) 18
Hollis, Louise (U.S.A.) 26
horse-dung sculpture 9
Hostetler, Mark (U.S.A.) 9
house, mountain bike race
    through 22
hugging T-shirts 23

I
ice sculpture 22
insects
    eating locusts 32, 32
    identifying splats on cars
        9
    spitting dead crickets 23
insurance, against ghosts 30
intravenous feeding 33

J
jack o'lantern carving 19, 19
Jarrett, Bill (U.S.A.) 9
Jenson, Jens (Den) 26
Jesus Christ
    image on frying pan 26
    image in water stain 33
Jo Jo "the Dog-faced Boy" 14, 14
Joachim, Suresh (Can) 32
John Paul II, Pope 16
Johnson, David "The Bushman"
    (U.S.A.) 30
Julie Andrée T. (Can) 19
Junguolong (Chn) 22, 22
junk art 10, 30

K
Katrencik, Emily (U.S.A.) 26
kite fighting 19
Klein, Calvin (U.S.A.) 32
knitting, sweaters for penguins
    23
Kusiek, Malissa (U.S.A.) 9, 9

L
Lanham, Moses (U.S.A.) 11, 11
leeches, severed ear reattached
    with help of 26
legless people
    legless and armless man
        23
    football player 18
    legless woman 9, 9
legs
    four-legged woman 23
    theft of artificial leg 22
Lincoln, Abraham, birthplace
    replica made of pennies
        25
liposuction
    self-administered 8
    soap made from fat 12
Liu Huirong (Chn) 30
locusts, eating 32, 32
Lou, Liza (U.S.A.) 8
love letters, building covered in
    10

M
Ma Chaoqin (Chn) 26, 26
McManus, Jim (Can) 26
McQueen, Willie (U.S.A.) 18
Madge, Sally (U.K.) 10
Margolles, Teresa (Mex) 32
marriage proposal, on fire 9, 9
    see also weddings
masks
    gatekeeper's 25
    theater 24
meat, face covered in raw 30
Meldrum, Pam (Can) 22
Mexico City, Ripley Museum 24,
    24–25
midgets
    baby-like 26, 26
    circus act 15, 15
    wedding 14, 14
Mikhalnichuk, Nikolai (Rus)
    29
Miller, Paul (U.S.A.) 32
Millner, Yvonne (U.S.A.) 32
Mochanou, Vasili (Can) 29
Mona Lisa, made from toast 24,
    24
money, Lincoln birthplace
    replica made of pennies 25
monkeys, smuggled on airplane
    33
Montandon, Adam (U.K.) 27
Mordrake, Edward (U.S.A.) 23
Morris, Peter (U.K.) 26
Motti, Gianni (Ita) 12
musical instruments, violin made
    from tombstone 26, 26
mustaches
    incentives to grow 30
    very long 32

N
Nagle, Matthew (U.S.A.) 10
nail polish, car decoration 32
necklace, crocodile tooth 24
needle, finding in haystack 15
Nematilaev, Alamjan (Kaz)
    26
nettles, World Stinging Nettle
    Eating Championships
    (U.K.) 28, 28–29
nipples
    lifting weights with 33, 33
    pulling cars with 33, 33
Nippulini, Great (U.S.A.) 33,
    33
nose
    drinking through 22, 22
    growing new nose on arm
        18
    two-nosed man 19

P
paintings, with cremation ashes
    10
Panfilov, Dimitrije (Yug) 8
Parra, Marcos (U.S.A.) 29
Pastrano, Juan (U.S.A.) 26

Paxton, Jeremy (U.K.) 18
Pecinovsky, John "half-and-half
    man" (U.S.A.) 14, 14
penguins, knitting sweaters for
    23
Perculeza, Albert M. and Karl
    Cedric (Phl) 10, 10
Perez Matos, Avelino (Cub) 14,
    14
performance art
    ambushes 30
    balloons 10
    battery chicken protest 22
    birth in public 19
    blindfold 19
    face covered in raw meat
        30
    gerbil 10
Perkins, Dr. Anna (U.S.A.) 12
Perry, Sarah (U.S.A.) 30
pets, dead pet-fur pillows 23
piercings, glasses attached to
    nose 18, 18
pigs
    pig-squealing championships
        12
    with house purchase 18
pillows, dead pet fur 23
pizza-smelling bathroom
    products 18
plastic surgery
    new nose 18
    self-administered liposuction
        8
playing cards, collecting in street
    15
Podesta, Paola (Chl) 28
poisons, snake venom injections
    28
poltergeists, insurance against
    30
pregnancy
    baby developing in mother's
        liver 8
    woman gives birth to frog 26
Price, Dr. William (U.K.) 12
Pritchard, Doug (U.S.A.) 26
pumpkins
    jack o'lantern carving 19, 19
    pumpkin festival 19

R
rabbit, giant sculpture of 18
Raghavendra, R.S. (Ind) 12, 12
Randian, Prince "The Living
    Torso" (B.Guy) 23
religious images
    Jesus Christ on frying pan 26
    Jesus Christ in water stain
        33
    Virgin Mary in underpass 16,
        16
Relles, Steve (U.S.A.) 28
restaurants
    slow food 10
Rich, Lucky (Aus) 13, 13
Rieti (Ita), washtub race 19

Rigo, Jeffrey (U.S.A.) 33
rings, engraved with heartbeats
    12
Ripley Museum, Mexico City 24,
    24–25
Rivera, Gabriela (Chl) 30
robots
    camel race 23
    suit for extra strength 18, 18
rock rat, discovery of 16
rocking chair, nonstop marathon
    32
rodent, new species discovered
    16
Rogers, Jim (Can) 9
root carving 25
Rosella, Francesca (Ita) 23
Roussel, Olivier and Yohann
    (Fra) 12
Rubottom, Ezekiel (U.S.A.) 9

S
Schmidt, Agnes (U.S.A.) 15, 15
Scott, James (U.S.A.) 33
scuba diving, dog (U.S.A.) 16
sculpture
    balloons 18
    bones 30
    chewing gum art 23
    cutlery 24
    horse dung 9
    giant beaver 18
    ice 22
    junk art 10, 30
    junk elephant 22
    tree root carving 25
shaving in space 18
Shea, Chaucey (Can) 9
shoes, hanging from tree 8, 8
Siamese twins 15, 15
    four-legged woman 23
    two-faced man 23
signatures, forged 9
skin
    peeling off 16
    rubber 15, 15
skeletons, whale's 25
sleep store, in shopping-center
    23
Smith, Daniel Browning (U.S.A.)
    31, 31
smoking, armless and legless
    man 23
snails, plastic snails glued to
    church 28
snakes
    eating 16
    found in egg 28
    venom injections 28
snowballs, Canadian Flag replica
    29
soap, made from body fat 12
Sooy, James (U.S.A.) 18, 18
Sordie, Tom (U.K.) 15, 15
Sparre, Nina (Swe) 32
spitting dead crickets 23
sport see extreme sports

Stevens, Dalton (U.S.A.) 12, 12
straitjacket, escapologist (U.S.A.) 20, 21
surgery see plastic surgery
sword swallowing
   by belly dancer 17, 17
   multiple swords 17, 21, 21

T

T-shirts, hugging 23
Takahashi, Tomoko (Jap) 10
tattoos, on back of head 23, 23
teeth
   crocodile tooth necklace 24
   growing in foot 26
   lifting weights with 13
   strengthened 13, 13
Thompson, Rob (Can) 22
thorns, large number removed from body 26
thumb, replaced with big toe 26
time capsule, car buried in 23
Timmins, Robert (U.S.A.) 16
toast, Mona Lisa made from 24, 24
"Tocci" twins (Ita) 15, 15
toenails, very long 26
toes
   extra 10, 10
   thumb replaced with big toe 26
toilet paper
   Beatles memorabilia 8, 8
   large collection of 9
toiletries, pizza-smelling 18
"Tom Thumb, General" (U.S.A.) 14, 14
Tomaini, Jeanie (U.S.A.) 9, 9
tombstone, violin made from 26, 26
tongues
   dexterity 25
   forked 30, 30
   hammering nail through 20, 21
trees
   root carving 25
   roots in coffin 22
   shoes hanging from 8, 8

turtles
   fiberglass shell 10
   smuggled onto airplane 29
twins
   parasitic fetus 26
   see also Siamese twins

U

Unarrom, Kirriwat (Tha) 6, 6–7

V

Valentine's Day, birds choosing mates on 22
Verhill, Didier (Bel) 12
Veruschka, Natasha (U.S.A.) 17, 17
Vesanen-Laukkanen, Virpi (Fin) 19, 19
violin, made from tombstone 26, 26
Virgin Mary, image in underpass 16, 16

W

wall, eating 26
Warren, Lavinia (U.S.A.) 14, 14
washtub race 19
weddings
   freak show 9
   heartbeats engraved on rings 12
   midgets 14, 14
weights
   lifting with nipples 33, 33
   lifting with teeth 13
whale skeleton 25
Wheeler, Vivian (U.S.A.) 8
Widenfalk, Lars (Swe) 26, 26
Williams, Roger (U.S.A.) 22
Wilson, Ben (U.K.) 23
Witt, Winfried (Ger) 19
Wolf, Eric (Can) 22
wrists, flexible (Ind) 12, 12
writing, simultaneously with both hands (Ind) 33

X

X-ray vision (Russia) 22, 22

Y

Yeargain, Sarah (U.S.A.) 16
Yusuf, Madina (Nig) 18

ACKNOWLEDGMENTS

COVER (t/r) Moses Lanham, (b/r) Natasha Veruschka, (b/l) Jim McNitt; 4 CLY Creation; 6 (c/l) Chaiwat Subprasom/Reuters, (r) Leon Schadeberg/Rex Features; 7 (l) Leon Schadeberg/Rex Features, (r) Chaiwat Subprasom/Reuters; 8 (t) Ben Phillips/Barcroft Media, (b) Craig Barritt/Barcroft Media; 9 (t) Malissa Kusiek/Empics, (b) Mark Mirko/Rex Features; 11 Moses Lanham; 12 (t) Indranil Mukherjee/AFP/Getty Images; 13 Will Burgess/Reuters; 16 (t) Barcroft Media, (b) John Gress/Reuters; 17 Natasha Veruschka; 18 (t) Camera Press/ED/JM, (b) Kimimasa Mayama/Reuters; 19 (t) Francois Lenoir/Reuters, (b) Alexander Demianchuk/Reuters; 20–21 (dp) Jim McNitt; 20 (b/l) Jim McNitt; 21 (b/c) Jim McNitt, (b/r) CLY Creation; 22 (t) Photoex/Ma Qibing/Camera Press, (b) Stuart Clarke/Rex Features; 23 Kai Pfaffenbach/Reuters; 26 (t) Chinafotopress/Camera Press, (b) Gary Roberts/Rex Features; 27 Simon Burt/Rex Features; 28–29 Ian Patrick/Rex Features; 29 Doug Hall/Rex Features; 30 (t) Chip East/Reuters, (b) Claro Cortes IV/Reuters; 31 Wierzbicki/BEI/Rex Features; 32 Ben Phillips/Barcroft Media; 33 (t/l & t/r) Heather Insogna, (b) Toby Melville/Reuters

All other photos are from Corel, PhotoDisc, Digital Vision and Ripley's Entertainment Inc.